For Your Garden

WATER GARDENS

For Your Garden

WATER GARDENS

Carol Spier

FRIEDMAN/FAIRFAX
PUBLISHERS

A FRIEDMAN/FAIRFAX BOOK

© 1993 by Michael Friedman Publishing Group, Inc.

Library of Congress Cataloging-in-Publication Data available upon request.

ISBN 1-56799-272-2

Editor: Kelly Matthews
Art Directors: Jeff Batzli and Lynne Yeamans
Designer: Stan Stanski
Photography Director: Christopher C. Bain

Printed in China by Leefung-Asco Printers Ltd.

For bulk purchases and special sales, please contact:
Friedman/Fairfax Publishers
Attention: Sales Department
15 West 26th Street
New York, New York 10010
212/685-6610   FAX 212/685-1307

Table of Contents

INTRODUCTION

To think of a water garden is to envision a glassy pond padded with flat green lily leaves and roseate blooms, sharp iris blades piercing here and there through the sun-dappled surface, and perhaps, the bright flash of a goldfish darting in and out of duckweed shadows or a moss-covered fountain rippling the surface with graceful arcs of water. Water gardens seem inevitably to whisper of magic, hint at mystery, and tease the senses with delight—perhaps because the water, which is so crucial to all plant and animal life, takes on a life of its own, catching the light of the sun and moon, stirring under the wind or rain, and reflecting and echoing the foliage, architecture, and clouds that frame it.

Water gardens can be designed in any size or shape, and any landscape plan can be enhanced by one. Water gardens (or planted pools or ponds—the terms are interchangeable but all refer to bodies of water in which some form of vegetation is growing) can be small or large, sunken permanently in the ground or set above it in a tublike container. They can be regular and geometric in shape or free-form and organic. They can have clean edges and an orderly arrangement of plants, which will give them a formal appearance, or they may be casually arranged, perhaps edged with rocks softened by cascading vegetation and planted in an apparently haphazard manner, which will give them a naturalistic or infor-

mal appearance. They can play a dominant role in the landscape's design, assuming a central or focal position, or they can be placed discreetly, providing an element of surprise each time they are discovered.

INTEGRATING A WATER GARDEN WITH YOUR LANDSCAPE

The particulars of water garden design will be dictated by individual circumstances—the size of your yard, the climate in which you live, and the amount of time and money you wish to invest—but you can design a garden that is as sedate or exuberant as you desire. Devote some thought to the architectural style of your home and to any landscaping that already exists so that your garden can be integrated successfully, decide whether you want a prominent or secluded pool, and then give your imagination, whim, and fancy free reign.

ABOVE LEFT: This long, narrow lily pond set in a hedge-enclosed garden is formal but mysterious. The rows of plane trees create a secluded environment that is enhanced by the secret chamber tucked in under the double stairway. An ivy-covered mount such as this may be absolutely artificial but lends a wonderful feeling of antiquity to the setting and provides a lovely vantage point for contemplation, as do the benches at the edge of the green.

OPPOSITE: A groomed and manicured parklike setting is the classic environment for a large formal water garden. This one has a modified cruciform and is sparsely planted; the regular, controlled arrangement of shrubbery and flower pots is mirrored on the clean expanse of water. The overall landscape is flat and rectilinear within an evergreen frame; low-clipped boxwood parterres outline beds planted with blocks of blooming seasonal color and lead onto an expanse of lawn. The flat stone pond surround is a frame within a frame; the water garden itself provides an elegant focal point that is punctuated by the upright clumps of irises and the silver mounds at each corner.

RIGHT: Water gardens need not be part of a formal vista. Here, an irregularly curved pond spills out of an herbal border just a few steps from the house. Carved into the bank of a stream that meanders across the property, this pond is edged with flat native stone and planted with a few lilies. The effect is gentle and subdued: the cool green and silver vegetation contrasts with the warm brick and stone, the assorted textures complement the rustic setting, and the smooth water trails informally into the passing stream.

LEFT: This paisleylike pond breaks up a long, narrow yard, which is walled in by evergreens that at first glance give the garden a formal appearance. In fact, the plantings curve, spill, and meander through the space with contrived naturalism. The curves make the space less narrow and lead the eye pleasantly through the three distinct sections of the landscape.

OPPOSITE: The irregular stones that form the bank of this rectilinear water garden are softened with tufts of greenery and bordered by pebbled paths, giving it the appearance of a natural stream. The large terra-cotta urns that dot the verges make a nod toward formality, but the confines of the garden, the rocky edging, and the sprays of daylilies have an aura of disorder that is charming and casual.

OPPOSITE: This beautiful round lily pond is set between a rolling lawn and a lovely perennial border. The sharp grassy edge and elegant bench lend the setting formality while the rocky shore and lush foliage provide a naturalistic balance; this yard is large enough for such a transition to be made without effort. The small statue appears to be contemplating the charm of her reflection in the pond.

TOP RIGHT: In a confined garden, a tiny planted pond can elicit a smile of pleasure each time it is discovered. This small walled garden is really no more than a narrow pathway along the side of the house, but it has been carefully planted with well-proportioned shrubs, perennials, and annuals. The curving pattern of the brickwork widens the space and invites the eye to search for details. The water garden is an organically shaped pond with one boggy edge that allows a variety of moisture-loving plants to thrive—and mask the water with a bit of green secrecy. If you live in an urban or town house environment where yards are small, you might contemplate a garden such as this.

BOTTOM RIGHT: A small water garden can provide a focal point in a small garden as effectively as in a large parklike one. This walled garden is very serene; the woven brick pattern and concentric right angles are formal but not austere. The importance of the pond in the center of this primarily shady space is emphasized as it catches the passing rays of the sun and moon. In a small space such as this, simple plantings in a limited palette enhance the quiet, serene mood, as do the terra-cotta animals that pose with everlasting and whimsical concentration.

ABOVE: A raised water garden brings its charms closer to hand, particularly if it is built with broad walls that beckon the visitor to come and sit alongside. In this case, a multilevel raised pool forms part of a border that surrounds a small lawn. The gardens here are fabulous, lush, and colorful, and although the pool is massive, its proportions are balanced by the tall ornamental grass, the exuberant roses, and the broad floral borders. The stone terrace, veined with creeping greens, helps to ease the transition from water garden to floral borders, and bits of stone wall add needed weight to the opposite edge of the lawn.

OPPOSITE: There is no reason not to tuck a tiny water garden into a deep floral border. Here, one is half-hidden by greens and blooms, which comes as a lovely surprise when discovered while strolling along the garden path. The rocks that surround this pool have a marvelously textured surface that is complemented by the dappled water and dense lily pads, and the pool, tucked amid lavishly planted stock, poppies, delphiniums, ivy, and ferns, is intimate.

ABOVE: A round formal garden very often features radiating pathways framing beds of massed plantings. On this brick terrace, a lily pond takes the place of a central flower bed, contrasting but balancing the blocks of red and white impatiens. The effect is orderly and controlled, but the formal design is softened by the mossy surface of the bricks and the lavender that is growing at the water's edge.

OPPOSITE: The use of small geometric beds set into a frame need not be limited to formal gardens. This charming garden features regularly shaped beds dropped somewhat casually into a lawn. The water garden in the foreground, with its sloping brick border and cascading urns, is as well-worn as the the other beds, but in this garden, there is order within what first appears as disorder, and the overall effect is harmonious.

Chapter One

WATER GARDEN EDGINGS

*U*nless you happen to have a natural pond in your yard, the edging of your water garden will in all likelihood have to be set in place by you, but the material you use and the way in which you assemble it will give your garden a man-made or a natural-looking edge. Man-made edgings include those of preformed tubs or site-poured pools, which might be fiberglass or concrete or even the edge of a sunken wooden barrel, and also those that are permanently assembled of materials such as cut stone, concrete slabs, wood, or ceramic tile. Naturalistic edgings look as though they grew in place and may be created with landscaped vegetation, piled or scattered rocks, sand, mulch, pebbles, or a combination of these.

Man-made edgings are often, but not always, formal in appearance, while naturalistic edgings tend to be, but are not always, informal. A water garden's edging has as much or more effect upon the overall style of the garden as the plantings within it; it will be apparent through all seasons and should be compatible with the shape of the pond and complement your landscape design.

MAN-MADE EDGINGS

While all man-made pond edgings are hard to the touch, they may be smooth or highly textured, matte or shiny, and colored to blend or contrast with the water and foliage. Select your materials for the contribution they will make to the design of your garden, and consider whether they will enhance or compete with the vegetation or other elements of the setting.

ABOVE: Stone-edged and rectangular, this pond seems less austere than the one on the opposite page because it is tucked more intimately into its setting. Spiky daylily leaves spill over the stones to meld with massed waterlilies; taller spiky clumps of yucca rise at the end, their height echoed by a lovely wrought-iron gate that indicates that this is a private or secret place.

OPPOSITE: Here, stone slabs set in mortar border a formal pool. The clean edge of the stone cuts crisply against the grass and the glassy surface of the water and harmonizes with the lovely pergola at the far end. A great clump of yellow flag iris punctuates each corner of the pond and lilies float in graceful swathes across it. The design of this garden could not be more simple, but the space it occupies is grand; it is both serene and imposing.

ABOVE: An artfully constructed stone wall gives this water garden an informal, naturalistic appearance that belies the effort made to create it. The densely padded surface of the water, the irregularities of the stone wall, and the soft cascading greenery shot with colorful blooms are all textural elements that draw the eye in admiration.

ABOVE: Beautifully painted glazed ceramic tiles give this pool a formal look, but the setting, tucked amid dense shrubbery, is mysterious rather than mannered. The pool is lined with deep blue tiles, which intensify the reflected sky and foliage, and the anomalous rock formation and hunk of glass heighten the esoteric atmosphere. Tiles such as these command a lot of attention and may compete with or be lost in their surroundings; this pond is very simply planted so as to balance the busy setting.

ABOVE: A simple plank deck sits right over the edge of the soft liner of this informal water garden in the southwestern United States. The climate in this area is warm and dry, and the deck provides an easy, low-maintenance way to enjoy both sun and pond.

LANDSCAPED EDGINGS

As you select materials to use in a landscaped pond edging, consider the contrasts of height, color, and texture that are available in the hard elements you might use, such as rocks or sand, and in the vegetation that might grow at the shore. Visit your local nursery to find out what types of moisture-loving plants will thrive in your climate, and remember that while there are many plants that can grow in standing water, there are others that love the shallow, damp soil that might ring a pond or that can be planted in the crevices of a rock wall or terrace.

ABOVE: The pool in this formal garden is an extension of the elegant green in which it sits. The parklike space is broken only by the straight lines and planes of hedges and terraces; the beautifully groomed lawn rolls serenely to the water's edge, where the glint of sunlight and the texture of the lilies gently articulate the transition from lawn to pool. The edging of this pool, while made of grass, is one of several carefully contrived elements in the setting, and the effect is far from naturalistic.

ABOVE: Here is a water garden that looks as though it occurred naturally. Its edges are a bit ragged and punctuated by sprightly grasses and cattails; greenery seems to spill from water to shore and back again. This small pond sits between a lawn and a perennial border, where it offers a delightfully untidy surprise each time it is discovered.

OPPOSITE: This large woodland water garden could also be the work of Nature herself. The woods slope gently down to the far edge of the pond, where the shore is dotted with rocks. Moisture-loving forget-me-nots spread in carefree abandon over the mulched path along the left bank, which leads past an azalea before wandering into the wood. The pond itself blends into the shoreline with stands of irises and ornamental grasses.

RIGHT: Ponds edged with vegetation need not feel quite so abandoned as the one on the previous page. Here, irises, lilies, and moisture-loving grasses ring a small pond, but they in turn are bordered with irregular paving stones; the effect is naturalistic but contained.

LEFT: With marvelous stone terraced steps leading down to the lily pond, this setting relies on harmonious variations of color and texture for its charm; the terrace is veined with creeping herbs, a bank of mounding artemisia echoes the stony pattern, and small stone pools and beds of greenery meld the lily-dotted water with its surrounds.

OPPOSITE: Though tiny, this deep-set pond is arresting. Bordered with organically shaped rocks that are a bit out of scale for its size, the pond catches and draws the eye. The odd shape, rough rocks, pendulous evergreens, surprise of the spiking iris leaves, and darting of the fish all emphasize an intriguing lack of symmetry.

Chapter Two

RAISED WATER GARDENS

When a water garden is raised above ground level, it adds architectural as well as horticultural interest to your landscape. And of course, the closer the surface of the water is to the viewer's eye, the easier it is to admire. If the walls of a raised garden are broad enough, they can double as a delightful bench. The basins or pools that form raised water gardens are almost always preformed or sturdily constructed on site, so they tend to have a formal, rather than naturalistic, appearance. However, the style of the container, the way it is planted, and the setting in which it is placed can soften the look.

Raised water gardens are often quite small. They can be planted in purchased containers and set on a terrace or deck or partially submerged at a focal or hidden place in the yard. Larger raised water gardens are frequently placed at the center of a clearing or a formal garden, or integrated with a paved terrace.

ABOVE: A lily pond at the center of this intimate clearing is an excuse to indulge in quiet contemplation. The slightly raised pond is smooth, round, and serene; it is the perfect enhancement for a classic setting like this, where the stone bench, blooming santolina, and graveled path contribute to the cloistered mood.

OPPOSITE: This oval water garden links the terrace of an elegant waterside home with a small lawn and complements the natural expanse of water below. Although imposing by virtue of its size and setting, it is very simply planted with containers of ornamental grass and appears contemporary and unfussy.

ABOVE: This pitted stone urn has perhaps graced the center of this perfectly paved terrace for most of remembered time. When the seasons smile upon them, the lilies and grass within it make a small show of splendor; otherwise they fade into antiquity with their environment.

RIGHT: It can be difficult to successfully integrate diverse elements in a small space, but here, squares and rectangles and wood, brick, and stone have been carefully arranged to create an inviting walled retreat. With no real room for a bench in this garden, the raised pond offers a surprising and pleasant place to rest. The little geyser fountain lightens the pond and echoes the wonderful tall stalks of digitalis and the posts of the lattice; the eye moves up and around to enjoy the space.

ABOVE: Placed in the middle of a sunny terrace, the pentagonal walls of this water garden make an unusual and rather formal frame for the casual planting within. Bright white in the sunlight, the stone slabs stand in stark but not displeasing contrast to the water, rock, and greenery.

ABOVE: Fieldstones embedded in concrete give this raised pond a rugged, rustic look that would complement a Craftsman-style house—or any vernacular stone dwelling. Although the slender lines of the formal white bench seem oddly juxtaposed with such a heavy pond, the gardens are robust and provide a good balance.

ABOVE: A show-off container such as this bronze basin will look most effective if it is planted quietly. White blooms set against green leaves are an elegant choice to crown the patina-masked relief of the basin, particularly when placed, as it is here, within formal white walls.

RIGHT: Raised water gardens—like sunken ones—can be tucked into beds and borders for an element of surprise or mystery. Even in a very small space, such as the corner of this walled garden, a little planted pond can be a great discovery. Nestled beneath small rhododendrons, this one—complete with goldfish and duckweed—is a common half-barrel of the type available at any nursery. As in some Japanese gardens, the ground has been covered with pebbles, which provide a lovely setting for the variegated foliage above.

ABOVE: If a raised water garden is small enough, it can be placed among other potted plants. This one, in a green basin, has been topped with a sheet of glass (note the spacers that allow air to reach the garden) to make a witty outdoor end table for a patio.

OPPOSITE: When a raised water garden is set amid lively vegetation, it begins to look as naturalistic as a sunken pond with overgrown edges. Here, an exuberant flower bed embraces a rather small pond, the quiet water set off by a profusion of purple and the happy birdhouse that stands guard.

Chapter Three

MOVING WATER

*W*hile still water provides a glassy surface that turns a water garden into a reflecting pool with a serene or austere character, moving water adds a touch of grace, frivolity, or sensuality. Just as ocean waves or river currents mesmerize the passerby, a fountain spray that arcs in rainbow droplets or an ever-changing waterfall cause one to pause and pass into reverie. Moving water, whether quietly flowing or playfully dancing, is somehow irresistible.

Water can flow through a planted pool in the manner of a stream, perhaps cascading over several terraced levels, or it can spout, spray, bubble, or trickle above it through a fountain. Unless you are planting an existing streambed or natural spring, you will need to install an electric pump for circulation. A fountain itself can be sculptural, elaborate and showy, or simple and unobtrusive; a waterfall or cascade can course over rocks or steps, puddling in basins as it moves, or slide down the surface of a retaining wall. Fountains, particularly sculptural ones or those that spray above the water's surface, usually bring a note of formality; cascades and falls may or may not be formal, depending upon the situation. Various styles of fountains are associated with different periods of garden history and with European, Middle Eastern, and Oriental garden styles; when selecting a fountain, you may find it interesting to do some research. A fountain should complement the ambience of its setting; one that is pretentious or incongruous will cheapen rather than enhance the design.

FOUNTAINS

OPPOSITE: The pergola behind this lily pool forms one end of the walled flower garden at Old Westbury Gardens on Long Island. Plumes of water spray in arcs that echo those of the framework beyond; the fountain—a child holding an urn above its head—is diminutive and in proportion with the lilies.

ABOVE: Although the gloriously glazed blue basin that bubbles in the center of this small pool is rather large, its simple shape and gently flowing water settle it into the round frame of the surrounding garden. This setting is particularly beautiful with spring in full, glorious bloom.

ABOVE: A fountain placed to one side of a water garden will have the effect of perpetually filling the pool. If the fountain is sculptural, this narrative quality will be enhanced; here, a satyr, standing appropriately upon a small mound of ivy, pipes water into a quiet garden through his double flute.

LEFT: In an informal water garden, simple jets of water rising magically above the pond's surface may be all that is needed in the way of a fountain. By selecting a fountain that sprays from an invisible source, the design stays simple and uncluttered; here, the shape of the spray repeats that of the foliage.

ABOVE: There is nothing to prevent you from installing a decorative fountain in the tiniest of water gardens; just be sure that it is in proportion to the space. This small pond sits at the base of an old brick wall, which provides the perfect mount for a spouting lion's head. The choice of colors and materials is harmonious so the fountain comes as a pleasant but appropriate surprise.

LEFT: Usually set off by the spare formality of Japanese gardens, a trickling fountain seems equally at home in this naturalistic lily pool settled into the lush background of New Zealand foliage. The simple horizontal pipe is cast to replicate bamboo, and water flows through it into a spherical stone basin, which fills and glistens continuously from the overflow. Here, the fountain is eased into its setting by the large spherical finial topping the stone post and echoed in subtle reflection in the pool.

ABOVE: If your water garden is designed with a sense of mystery, perhaps hidden in a shady, over-grown corner, you might want it to summon passersby with the sound, but not the sight, of moving water. A submerged fountain that bubbles just below the surface would be quietly intriguing; you might build a very simple one that springs up from underwater rocks or choose one that tells an eerie tale.

FALLING WATER

ABOVE: The synthetic antiquity of this decaying wall gives focus and importance to a small pool of irises. Piped water overflows from each perfectly tilted terra-cotta vessel to stream slowly into the pool below. The design, while completely contrived and certainly not appropriate to every landscape, is a marvelous juxtaposition of naturalistic elements in a structured setting.

OVERLEAF: Water spills down this magnificent procession of round cast-iron basins into a series of round stone-rimmed pools, making its entry like royalty proceeding down a grand stairway. A garden such as this certainly owes much of its impact to its impressive proportions, but the design is particularly effective because it relies upon the repetition of just a few well-chosen elements.

ABOVE: If you so desire, Nature's hand can be supplemented by your own to tame a wilderness proper-ty. The bed of this naturally falling stream has been helped to step down into a pool, and over time, the rocks and pools have grown into the setting, so that there is a feeling of pleasure, but not surprise, when one happens upon the stream.

OPPOSITE: The watery steps that lead to this lily pond take advantage of a natural slope in the land-scape. This is an intimate cascade, its rocky steps softened with water-loving plants and its banks filled with shrubs and perennials; while the scene is charmingly natural, the reality was lovingly contrived.

Chapter Four

WATER GARDENS IN BLOOM

*I*f you are planning a water garden, you must of course think not only of the size and shape of the pool and the way it is constructed but also of the plants that will fill it. Indeed, your love of water lilies or Japanese irises might inspire you to create a water garden before you even think of the particulars of the pool itself. The specific plants you are able to grow in your pond and at its edges will be dictated in part by the climate and location in which you live, but there are many species that can be considered—and loved—for the color, shape, texture, and attitude they contribute.

Because most plants have a limited season of glory, it is a good idea to conceive the basic style and construction of your pond so that it will be attractive no matter what the time of year and then select appropriate plants as you would for any other part of your garden, choosing them to carry out a theme, provide continuous bloom, create a particular palette, or thrive with minimum care, as desired. If your water garden is part of a larger garden, make sure its design relates to its environment—the surrounding plants can set off or extend its beauty.

RIGHT: Early summer, with its profusion of blooms, is a lovely time for any garden. For the water gardener, it is the season of the Japanese iris. In this garden, there is a wonderful juxtaposition of elegant and robust blooms with exotic foliage.

OPPOSITE: The plantings in this garden are massed so that each makes a strong statement of shape and color. The water lilies will not bloom until later in the season, but their leaves carpet the surface of the pond with green, the purple blooms of the irises punctuate their spiky foliage, and a great drift of red euphorbia leads the eye to the mounds of greenery beyond.

OVERLEAF: Perennial candelabra-type primroses thrive in moist soil and light shade. Their bright springtime blooms are festive yet delicate at the edge of a naturalistic pond.

ABOVE: These two views of a Shropshire garden in summer reveal a pretty pond bordered by showy perennials. A variety of shapes and textures assures that when the blooms have faded the border will retain its interest.

OPPOSITE: Lovely daylilies, which grow wild along so many rural roadsides, lend an old-fashioned, country-fresh feeling to the edge of a water garden. Here, they make an informal transition from rolling lawn to stony shore. There are hundreds of varieties of daylilies; they come in myriad colors and sizes and are easy to establish, spreading quickly to make beds of dancing blooms.

ABOVE: It is not only the glassy surface of water that fascinates. In this small shallow pool, the water is completely obscured by tightly textured foliage that forms an intriguing monochromatic carpet. Punctuated with unusual rocks and tightly contained within its frame, the pond assumes the importance of a piece of sculpture.

LEFT: Textural interest can also be created in a small water garden when you fill it with remarkably disparate plants. Each specimen planted in this tiny barrel is a different shape, size, and texture; the effect is lively and charming.

OPPOSITE: Massed plantings of a single species, intense with repeated shape and color, are often more impressive than random plantings of several interspersed varieties. Here, a band of pickerel weed, with its bright blue flower spikes and heart-shaped leaves dancing in the sun, cuts without affectation across one end of a casual water garden.

ABOVE: Simple symmetrical plantings, which emphasize the regularity of a pond's outline, are an enhancement to a formal water garden, particularly if it is set imposingly within an open lawn or courtyard. Lilies planted in submerged tubs float in controlled rounds of color in each branch of this pool; the formality is continued by the even placement of the urns on the terrace.

RIGHT: Technically speaking, a water garden is a pond in which submerged or floating plants are growing, but if you are not prepared to establish the real thing, you can easily grow a cheater's version without sacrificing any charm. Here, a wire basket is filled to overflowing with summery annuals and then perched atop a pile of stones, where it sits as a cheery filip to a natural stream.

OPPOSITE: When a very small water garden is incorporated into a larger garden, as this one is into a flower border, it should be viewed as just one design element among several. This garden, which is planted with charming old-fashioned flowers, is unified with a few rustic props—the trellis, the tree stump, and the rock ledge around the little pond.

ABOVE LEFT: Naturalistic lily ponds with heavily landscaped verges provide a wonderful opportunity for textural garden composition. Here, massed floating lily leaves carpet the surface but allow glinting light to bounce between them; the foliage along the shore is variously and delicately cut, contrasting gently with the full roundness of the lily pads below.

ABOVE RIGHT: An intense band of pink begonias strengthens the outline of a formal pool. Here, urns of nasturtiums and petunias unite and extend the bright colors of pond and border.

OPPOSITE: Even though the foliage spills into this pond in a continuous green flow, there is a marked textural contrast between the lily pads and landscaping in this subtropical climate. The deeply cut, arching fronds of ferns and palms, dotted brightly with daylilies and fuchsia, extend an exotic, exuberant embrace like a great ruffled collar around the smooth swathe of lilies.

Chapter Five

SPECIAL TOUCHES

*A*ll but the most utilitarian gardening is a form of decorating and therefore owes its ultimate aesthetic success to the designer's finishing touches. Certainly a garden may be unaccessorized and still be beautifully complete, but objects made by human—rather than Nature's—hands can add charm, create mood or narrative interest, or importantly, provide structural support or access. Finishing touches for a water garden might take the form of statuary or small sculpture, a bridge to cross the pool, or even stepping stones to place one amid the lilies.

STATUARY

Water garden statuary often represents figures from antiquity that are associated with water or water-dwelling creatures. It can be life-size, smaller or larger, prominently displayed or hidden among the foliage. Stone, ceramic, and metal pieces that are not sealed or glazed will weather over time and grow a patina that will blend with their surroundings, heightening the sense of mystery that so often pervades a water garden.

ABOVE: Here, a water garden is set into a niche in a garden wall, making a damp and shady grotto. A triton (merman) fills the space and points the way to other wonders through a stand of ferns. A niche such as this would command attention even without the statue, but it begs to frame a composition of some importance.

OPPOSITE: A single statue placed at the center of a formal pool draws the eye and initiates a drama for its setting. The maid in the center of the pond is perhaps a naiad, a fresh-water nymph, caught forever gazing into the depths of the pool before stooping to fill the vessels in her arms.

ABOVE: Realistically proportioned animal sculptures can catch the casual observer off-guard with their unnatural stillness. Two doves have stopped for a meal in the middle of this raised garden and a turtle stands with typical torpor where the water breaks over the wall.

LEFT: It takes a good eye to judge proportion when you are placing statuary, but you may find that realism can successfully give way to whimsy. This fish is of course much too large to inhabit the tiny pool from which he springs, and though the frog who watches from among the petunias seems quite shocked to see him, he brings a smile to the human observer, as does the diminutive, verdigris rabbit poised atop a spray of leaves.

ABOVE: The heron is an elegant water bird known for its stealthy walk and patient stance when searching for food. Herons are classic garden ornaments and are readily available from garden furnishings catalogs. This specimen stands quite realistically at the edge of a naturalistic pond.

ABOVE: Sculptural ornaments need not be representational. You might choose a piece that is abstract or use an organic object such as driftwood. You might also select a functional object with pleasing proportions. The water garden set against this low wall is edged with assorted stones. The large stone at the back is a hand-hollowed slab, and the stone basin that sits on it has a simple, pleasing shape. The composition is spare and soothing yet has a quiet intensity as the repeated rounds and hollows draw and hold the eye.

ABOVE: The serenity of this circular pool is enhanced by the muted natural tones of the statue that stands at its center. The juxtaposition of the vividly colored flowers surrounding this calm body of water creates a lovely counterpoint.

LEFT: The placement of this statue by the edge of a free-form pond emphasizes the intimacy of this water garden setting. Here, a long-haired maid relaxes in privacy, leisurely wringing her hair as if she had just emerged from the water.

BRIDGES AND STEPPING STONES

Bridges and stepping stones are functional embellishments that make a water garden easier to enjoy. If your water garden is shaped in such a way that it invites you to explore the opposite shore or walk among the plantings, a bridge or a path of stones will bring you closer to its beauty. Stepping stones can be formally arranged, but they are most often used in naturalistic settings. Bridges can be architecturally impressive or intensely colored, standing in contrast to the plantings, or simple and unobtrusive, blending with the environment. As is true of fountains, there are particular types of bridges that are associated with certain styles and periods of garden design, and you might find it rewarding to study them in some detail before going to the trouble of building one.

ABOVE: Camelback bridges are characteristic features of Oriental gardens, where they not only link one area with another but also provide strategic vantage points for admiring the space and proportions of the garden. The bright red color is typical of bridges built in the Heian period (710–1150) in Japan; this one is quite large.

OPPOSITE: Nature no doubt intended that streams should be crossed; if you are lucky enough to have one as pleasant as this meandering through your yard, you will of course want to reach the other side with ease. The banks of this stream have the look of a cottage garden; the bridge that links them is an unpretentious plank arc that will be softened as it weathers with the passage of time.

ABOVE: Giverny, the home of Claude Monet, has one of the best loved and most famous of domestic water gardens. Monet was very much influenced by what he knew of Japanese gardens when he designed his water garden, and it has a marvelous blend of Oriental and French features. The gently arced bridge at the far end is covered with a wisteria arbor.

OPPOSITE: Zigzag bridges are typical of Oriental gardens, where they are placed just above the water to bring the visitor as close as possible to important plantings. This one is an inviting path amid spectacular Japanese irises.

ABOVE: There is something archaic and appealing about this disheveled garden. Informal access to the plants and assorted pedestals is provided by the stone slab that spans the water and the stepping stones that wander along the shore.

LEFT: In this naturalistic garden, slabs of slate appear to float across the pond. The effect is slightly unnerving but rather magical, inviting one to watch one's step—and admire the water.

OPPOSITE: Stepping stones are not often seen in formal water gardens, but in the right context, they can be used to make an orderly path along an edge or from one area to another. This wonderful sunken pond sits well below a lush floral border. The steps that lead to the pool, while not grand, have a certain majesty, and the regular stones that rim the perimeter offer a nearly irresistible access to the water.